HOW It's MADE

A Rubber Tire

Sarah Ridley

GARETH**STEVENS**
GS

P U B L I S H I N G

A Member of the WRC Media Family of Companies

The publishers would like to thank Michelin and Goodyear Dunlop for their help with this book.

Please visit our web site at: **www.garethstevens.com**
For a free color catalog describing Gareth Stevens Publishing's list of high-quality books
and multimedia programs, call 1-800-542-2595 (USA) or 1-800-387-3178 (Canada).
Gareth Stevens Publishing's fax: (414) 332-3567.

Library of Congress Cataloging-in-Publication Data

Ridley, Sarah, 1963- .
     A rubber tire / Sarah Ridley.
        p. cm. – (How it's made)
     Includes index.
     ISBN 0-8368-6295-3 (lib. bdg.)
     1. Tires–Juvenile literature.   2. Rubber–Juvenile literature.   I. Title.
TS1912.R53   2006
678'.32–dc22   2005054073

This North American edition first published in 2006 by
Gareth Stevens Publishing
A Member of the WRC Media Family of Companies
330 West Olive Street, Suite 100
Milwaukee, WI 53212 USA

This U.S. edition copyright © 2006 by Gareth Stevens, Inc.
Original edition copyright © 2005 by Franklin Watts.
First published in Great Britain in 2005 by Franklin Watts,
96 Leonard Street, London EC2A 4XD United Kingdom

Series editor: Sarah Peutrill
Art director: Jonathan Hair
Designer: Jemima Lumley

Gareth Stevens editor: Barbara Kiely Miller
Gareth Stevens art direction: Tammy West
Gareth Stevens graphic designer: Charlie Dahl

Photo credits: (t = top, b = bottom, l = left, r = right, c = center)
Richard Anthony/Holt Studios: 30b. Nigel Cattlin/Holt Studios: 6bl. Courtesy of John Deere: 25b. Digital Vision: 12bl, 12tr. Mary
Evans Picture Library: 9b. Courtesy of Goodyear Dunlop: 20, 22, 27tl, 27tr. Hulton Deutsch/Corbis: 13b. Philippa Lewis/Corbis:
15b. Tom & Dee McCarthy/Corbis: 31. Michael Mathers/Still Pictures: 30t. Maximilian Stock Ltd/Science Photo Library: 15t, 16b,
24t, 27cr. Courtesy of Michelin: front cover (both), 1, 4t, 4b, 5r, 6tr, 11b, 14, 16t, 17t, 18, 21c, 25tr, 26tl, 26cl, 27bl, 27cl (both), back
cover (both). Shehzad Noorani/Still Pictures: 7, 8, 9t, 26bl, 26tr. Charles E. Rotkin/Corbis: 13t, 26br. Sipa Press/Rex Features: 23.
Robin Smith/Art Directors & Trip: 11t. Inga Spence/Holt Studios: 10, 26cr. Topham: 17b, 19t. Courtesy of Volkswagon Group: 24b,
27br. Watts: 19b, 28, 29. Larry Williams/Corbis: 21b.

Printed in the United States of America

1 2 3 4 5 6 7 8 9 10 09 08 07 06

Words that appear in the glossary are printed in
boldface type the first time they occur in the text.

Contents

A tire is made of rubber.

Making a tire starts with a rubber tree. The **sap** of a rubber tree contains natural rubber, which is called **latex**. Natural and **synthetic** rubber are the main materials in rubber tires.

Tires help make a car ride safe by smoothing out the bumps and gripping the surface of the road.

The latex from a rubber tree is tapped and collected in cups.

Rubber trees grow best in hot, wet **climates**. Most rubber trees grow on small, family-owned plantations, or farms. A small percentage of rubber trees come from large plantations with many trees.

Some of the main countries that produce rubber today are marked in green on this map.

New rubber trees start as seeds planted in pots and grown in greenhouses. The seeds grow into small plants called seedlings. When the seedlings are large enough, workers plant them outdoors in covered nursery beds. Finally, the young trees are planted in rows.

Why rubber?

Natural rubber, or latex, has amazing properties. One of the most important is elasticity. When rubber is stretched or bent, it springs back to its original shape. Elasticity is what makes rubber suitable for tires, because when tires roll over bumps, they bend out of shape and back into shape. Rubber's stretchiness also makes it perfect for all kinds of bouncing balls.

Scientists study seedlings (*above*) to learn which trees make the best latex. Rubber trees used to grow only in Brazil.

Plantation workers collect latex from rubber trees.

When rubber trees are six or seven years old, plantation workers called tappers take latex from the trees. Each tapper owns, or looks after, certain trees on the plantation.

Early each morning, the tapper cuts away a strip of bark half way around each tree trunk. A new cut is made just below any cut made before it. Like blood from a wound, the latex starts to flow and fills a collecting cup.

The tapper returns later that same day to collect the latex.

Latex flows from a tapped rubber tree.

A tapper on a rubber plantation slices away a strip of bark on the outside of a rubber tree to tap the latex inside.

The tapper empties the cups into a bucket and takes the latex to the local village. After a few hours, the cuts on the trees heal, and the latex stops flowing. The tapper will return to these trees in two or three days to tap them again.

Ma Than Than Htay (*see next page*) strains the latex collected from her rubber trees.

In the Past

In the 1800s, the British **empire** controlled a large part of the world. The British government set up **botanical** gardens in parts of the empire, including Sri Lanka, India, and Singapore. In these gardens, people began experimenting with rubber plants, which had previously been grown only in South America.

Henry Ridley, known as "Rubber" Ridley, was the director of the botanical garden in Singapore from 1888 to 1911. From the garden's twenty-two rubber tree seedlings, Ridley collected enough seeds to grow new plants for people interested in growing rubber trees in Malaysia. Ridley also developed better ways to tap rubber trees. His work helped establish a successful rubber industry in Asia.

The latex is made into sheets of rubber.

The collected latex is turned into rubber each day. Some plantations hire workers to do this job. Others are run as **cooperatives** or are run by families.

Ma Than Than Htay, who lives in Myanmar in Southeast Asia, owns twelve hundred rubber trees. With her family, she taps latex and makes it into sheets. First, she pours the latex into shallow trays. Then, she adds acid to the latex. The acid makes small lumps floating in the latex clump together. A thin layer of latex forms on the top of each tray.

Ma Than Than Htay pours creamy latex into shallow trays.

Workers lift the layers of latex out of the trays and feed them through rollers to squeeze out the water.

Ma Than Than Htay's sons help her feed latex through rollers to make sheets.

In the Past

Until about two hundred years ago, Native people living in the South American rain forest were the only people who tapped rubber trees. They made rubber capes, shoes, torches, and balls. To make rubber, they poured liquid latex onto a small ball of rubber attached to a stick. They held the stick over a smokey fire. The smoke and heat from the fire made the rubber in the latex harden and stick to the ball. More latex was added until the rubber ball became very large.

This nineteenth-century drawing shows how South American Natives made rubber.

Rubber tappers hang sheets of latex to dry.

Sheets of latex are hung like wet clothes on a line to dry.

The latex sheets are hung outdoors to dry. Then they are put in smokehouses, where heat from fires dry them even more. Workers hold each sheet of latex up to the light to check its quality. Sheets with the least dirt in them are worth the most money. The sheets are sorted by quality and packed into bales.

Some latex is **processed** in factories, where it goes through these same steps but on a larger scale. Other latex, however, is processed differently. Castor oil is dripped onto the sheets, making them break up into crumbs. The crumbs are dried and put in bags to be sold.

In factories, processing rubber is done on a bigger scale.

After processing, the latex can be shipped to tire factories, which use 70 percent of all the latex processed each year.

In the Past

The first air-filled car tire was invented by the Michelin brothers in 1895. Before then, many other people worked on tire designs, mostly for bicycles. In 1888, after watching his son struggling to ride a bicycle with solid rubber tires, John Boyd Dunlop had the idea of trapping air inside a rubber tire.

The French Michelin brothers amazed people in 1895 when they showed off their new air-filled tires on a car called the Eclair.

Synthetic rubber is made from oil.

A little more than half of the rubber used to make tires is synthetic. Synthetic rubber is made from oil and gas, rather than tree sap. Oil is found under the sea or in the ground.

Huge oil rigs remove oil from under the sea.

Oil is heated in tall towers at an oil refinery to separate it into its different parts.

The oil is collected and taken to oil refineries. There it is separated into different parts. Gasoline, diesel fuel, and waxy paraffin are taken out, leaving behind the parts of oil that can be made into synthetic rubber. This material goes to factories that make this kind of rubber.

Factories that make synthetic rubber treat the oil with chemicals, heat it to the right temperature, and mix it with natural gas. The result is a tough, stretchy substance that is a lot like natural rubber.

This synthetic rubber factory in Texas covers a wide area of land.

These women are moving the huge tires used for military vehicles in 1943.

In the Past

Scientists looking at natural rubber in the early 1900s found that they could make a similar material from oil products. By World War II (1939–1945), Germany, Russia, Great Britain, and the United States were making large amounts of synthetic rubber. The supply of synthetic rubber was enough to make tires for all the needed war vehicles at a time when it was difficult to obtain natural rubber from the other side of the world.

The rubber arrives at the tire factory.

Latex and synthetic rubber are about half of the ingredients needed to make a tire, but, altogether, about two hundred different materials are used. The latex and synthetic rubber are mixed with oil, **carbon black**, **silica**, **sulfur** and various chemicals. All of the ingredients are weighed and put into a huge mixer.

These are some of the many ingredients that make up a modern tire. They include oil, carbon black, rubber, steel wire, and silica.

In the mixer, the ingredients warm up and gradually turn into a smooth, thick liquid.

Scientists have learned how much of each material is needed to make a good tire.

Researchers work to find out which ingredients in a car tire will make it perform best. They use machines and computers to see how different tire materials stand up to use. They can test a computer-created tire more easily then using a real tire.

Why add to rubber?

Rubber is naturally tough and hard-wearing. The other ingredients scientists add to tires, however, make rubber last longer and resist wear and tear even more.

Early tires usually needed to be replaced after driving a car 450 to 900 miles (725 to 1,450 kilometers). Modern tires can last for more than 30,000 miles (48,000 km) before they are worn out.

Like many tire companies, Michelin developed a close tie with the sport of car racing, which showed off Michelin's tires. This picture of a 1907 race is displayed at a building in London that was Michelin's first British headquarters.

The rubber mixture is rolled into sheets.

After the final ingredients are added to the rubber mixture, it is pushed between the rollers of a milling machine and comes out the other side as sheets of flat, black rubber. The sheets are used to make different parts of a tire. Each part is made separately.

The sticky rubber mixture is pushed through a milling machine.

The rubber is checked at each step to make sure it will be high quality.

The Parts of a Tire

The tread band runs in a ring around a tire. The tread pattern helps the tire grip the road.

Steel wire is often mixed with rubber to form the belts on a tire. Belts give a tire added strength. They are located underneath the tire's tread.

The tire beads are steel wire pulled up tightly around each edge of a tire. They clamp the tire onto the wheel rim.

The body, or carcass, of a tire is a special kind of fabric that is made up of layers of rubber strengthened with synthetic or fabric cord.

The inside of a tire is a layer of airtight rubber.

The sidewalls are made of tough, flexible rubber to protect the sides of the tire.

In the Past

The Michelin man is one of the world's best-known images. He was created in 1898 when André Michelin noticed that a pile of tires could be made to look like a man by adding a head, arms, and legs. To show that Michelin tires were tough and would not **puncture** easily, the Michelin man was drawn with a big stomach, because he had eaten all the sharp objects, such as horseshoes, nails, and rocks, found on roads at that time.

Le pneu Michelin boit l'obstacle means "The Michelin tire drinks obstacles."

Machines produce the different parts of the tire.

In the factory, the rubber is placed into **molds** and squeezed through machines to produce shaped pieces.

The main parts of the tire are made by sandwiching metal or synthetic cords between sheets of rubber. Layers of these special fabrics build up the thickness and strength of the tire.

Cords are lined up on a machine before being sandwiched between rubber sheets to make the fabric for the carcass of the tire.

In the Past

In the early 1900s, it was more difficult to find good tires than good engines. Trips by car were often delayed because of punctured or blown out tires. Many drivers brought **mechanics** along on trips with them, mostly just to change the tires.

The owners of this car watch their mechanic fix one of the car's tires on the side of the road.

Why rubber?

Rubber is useful for making tires because it does not soak up water lying on the road. It is used to make many other products that need to be waterproof, too. Water runs off rubber gloves, protecting the hands inside from soapy water. Fabric is coated with a thin layer of rubber to make raincoats (*left*) and other waterproof clothes.

Factory workers put the parts of the tire together.

Each piece of the tire is placed, in order, on a metal drum. Workers start with an inner layer of airtight rubber. They lay rubber fabric on top of that. Each time another layer is added, air is pushed out.

Next, the tire beads are placed on the outside edges of the tire. Then, various strips of shaped rubber and the tire's sidewalls are placed in the correct positions. The belts and the tread band complete the tire.

A factory worker builds up the tire's layers on a metal drum, starting with the airtight rubber for the tire's inner layer.

At first, the tread band is smooth. Later, a pattern will be pressed into it. The most important job of a tire is to grip the road so a driver can steer and control the car. The tread pattern helps the tire do its job.

The tread patterns on tires are different, depending on the roads over which a car will be driven and the weather conditions in which the tires will be used.

In dry weather, race car drivers use almost smooth tires. At high speeds, the rubber in the tires becomes hot and sticky, which helps a race car grip the track.

The tire is heated in a mold.

The tire sits in a mold for about ten minutes while very hot water and steam heat its layers, sealing them together. The outside of the tire pushes against the walls of the mold, creating the tread design. This process, called curing, is done at about 300 °Fahrenheit (150 °Celsius).

Smooth tires (*on the left*) are about to go through the curing process. The top part of the molding machine will be lowered onto the bottom part.

In the Past

In places where temperatures range from very cold to hot, rubber products used to turn stiff in cold weather and sticky in hot weather. These changes kept people from buying products made of rubber. In 1841–1842, Charles Goodyear discovered that when he added sulfur to natural rubber and heated it, the rubber would stay in the same condition, regardless of the weather. This process became known as vulcanization.

During the curing process, the rubber is vulcanized. The heat in this step reacts with the sulfur in the tire to make the rubber stay in its final shape. Before vulcanizing was discovered, finished rubber products would change shape in hot or cold weather.

After a tire is released from the mold, it moves along a conveyor belt to be checked.

The quality of the tire is checked

As each tire comes out of its mold, it is checked for quality. This is the last step in a long line of checking and testing.

Computers and other machines test car tires at every step of manufacturing.

The tire is finally ready to be used on a vehicle.

Cars are just one type of vehicle that tires are used on.

Today, tires are made for all kinds of vehicles, from bicycles to space buggies and from racing cars to monster trucks and tractors. Each kind of tire is a different design and uses slightly different materials.

Tires on off-road cars have deep tread patterns that grip the ground, even in muddy conditions.

Look at the size of these tires! Huge tires spread a tractor's weight over a large area and stop the tractor from sinking into soft ground.

How a Rubber Tire Is Made

1. Rubber trees grow from seedlings. They take about six years to grow tall and strong.

4. The layers of latex are fed through rollers.

2. Rubber tappers slice into the bark of rubber trees to collect latex.

5. The sheets of latex hang on a line to dry.

3. The latex is poured into shallow containers where it forms a thin layer on top.

6. Synthetic rubber is made in a factory out of substances that come from oil.

10. The different parts of the tire are put together on a drum.

11. The tire is heated, or cured, in a mold.

9. Machines coat cords with rubber and make all the different parts of the tire.

12. The tire is tested.

8. The mixture goes through a milling machine to produce sheets of rubber.

7. Natural and synthetic rubber are mixed with about two hundred other ingredients.

13. The tire rolls off the conveyor belt, leaves the factory, and ends up on a car.

Rubber and Its Many Uses

Rubber is a very useful material. It is stretchy, tough, waterproof, grips well, and can be molded into different shapes. It is used for many items in our homes and in our world.

Rubber is used to erase pencil marks because it grips paper, and it picks up the carbon graphite material that the "lead" in pencils is made of.

Rubber is used to make hot water bottles because it is waterproof and holds in heat.

Because rubber bends and grips well, it covers the bottoms of athletic shoes. Some shoes even have treads, like tires.

Balloons made from rubber can stretch to enormous sizes.

Because rubber is waterproof, it is used to make coats, boots, and the wetsuits divers use for swimming in cold water.

Because electricity cannot flow through rubber, it is sometimes used to coat electric wires to make them safer.

Rubber is used on some things to create a seal, such as around the door of a clothes dryer or the lenses on a pair of swimming goggles.

Stretchy rubber bands are very useful for holding things together.

How many other uses for rubber can you think of?

Tires and the Environment

When tires wear out, they cause problems because they do not rot away. Millions of worn tires are thrown out each year, creating tire dumps around the world. Some ways have been found to solve this problem.

This sea of rubber is a tire dump in the United States.

Tire Research

Scientists working for tire companies test different materials and designs to find out which tires last the longest and help cars use less fuel. Sometimes, a tire can be given new tread, if the rest of the tire is not worn out. A truck tire can often be retreaded twice before it has to be replaced.

Tire companies also work with road builders to design tires that make less noise. The noise from tires can disturb people who live near busy roads.

If a tire is not too worn out, its tread can be replaced.

Drivers' Responsibility

Tires filled with the correct amount of air will last longer before they need replacing. Drivers should check the air in their tires often.

Reusing Tires

Used tires can be shredded and burned to provide energy for power stations, but the smoke from burning rubber is full of pollution so burning has to be done carefully. Some tires are broken down into powder that can be used to make other rubber items. Some of this powder is mixed with road surfacing materials to make new roads. Old tires can also be attached to the sides of docks to protect boats.

Old rubber tires make some of the best swings.

Glossary

botanical – having to do with plants

carbon black – a powdery black material made of carbon, which is a substance created when a material such as wood or coal burns

climates – areas of Earth with specific weather conditions, such as hot or cold or rainy or dry

cooperatives – businesses owned by and run for the benefit of the people using their services

empire – a group of countries and people ruled by one powerful country

latex – the milky juice of some plants that is the source of natural rubber

mechanics – people who fix machines

molds – containers that form shapes when liquid or soft materials, such as rubber, are poured or pressed into them and left to harden

processed – put through a series of steps or actions that lead to a result

puncture – to make a hole with something sharp

sap – the liquid that flows inside a plant, carrying food and water to its parts

silica – a form of sand

sulfur – a pale-yellow chemical

synthetic – not natural; made by people

Index